T0351436

New Letters to a Young Poet

New Letters to a Young Poet

JOAN MARGARIT

TRANSLATED BY CHRISTOPHER MAURER

SWAN ISLE PRESS
CHICAGO

Joan Margarit i Consarnau is a Catalan poet and architect and has won numerous awards for his previous books of poetry, most recently the Premio Nacional de Poesía for his *Casa de Misericordia*. Other works in English include *Tugs in the Fog* and *Mysteriously Happy*, both translated by Anna Crowe.

Christopher Maurer is professor of Spanish at Boston University. His translated works include Federico García Lorca's *In Search of Duende*; *The Complete Perfectionist: A Poetics of Work* by Juan Ramón Jiménez; and *Sebastian's Arrows: Letters and Mementos of Salvador Dalí and Federico García Lorca* (Swan Isle Press).

Swan Isle Press, Chicago 60640-8790

Edition©2010 by Swan Isle Press
©2010 by Joan Margarit
Translation©2010 by Christopher Maurer
All rights reserved. Published 2010. Printed in the United States of America

First Edition
14 13 12 11 10   12345
ISBN-13: 978-0-9748881-9-4 (cloth)

Originally published in the Catalan as *Noves cartes a un jove poeta*
© Raval Edicions, S.L.U., Proa, Barcelona, 2009
Peu de la Creu, 4, 08001 Barcelona
www.proa.cat

The Catalan text on which this translation is based has been licensed to Swan Isle Press by Raval Edicions, S.L.U., Proa, Barcelona.

Grateful acknowledgment to Fundació Gala-Salvador Dalí, and the Collection of the Salvador Dalí Museum, Inc., St. Petersburg, FL, 2010, for their respective permissions to use Salvador Dalí's painting, *The Basket of Bread,* for the jacket and interior illustration of *New Letters to a Young Poet: The Basket of Bread,* (1926), varnish medium painting on panel, 31.5 x 31.5 cm (12.40"x 12.40")
© Salvador Dalí. Fundació Gala-Salvador Dalí, (Artist Rights Society), 2010
©Salvador Dalí Museum, Inc., St Petersburg, FL, 2010

Library of Congress Cataloging-in-Publication Data

Margarit, Joan.
  [Noves cartes a un jove poeta. English]
  New letters to a young poet / Joan Margarit ; translated [from the Catalan] by Christopher Maurer. -- 1st ed.
      p. cm.
  Includes bibliographical references.
  ISBN 978-0-9748881-9-4 (alk. paper)
  1. Poetry. I. Maurer, Christopher. II. Title.
  PC3942.23.A6725N6813 2010
  808.1--dc22

                        2010042781

Swan Isle Press gratefully acknowledges that this book has been made possible, in part, with the support of generous grants from:

• Program for Cultural Cooperation between Spain's Ministry of Culture and United States Universities
• The Illinois Arts Council, A State of Illinois Agency
•Europe Bay Giving Trust

www.swanislepress.com

To Raquel, my one and only.

Contents

Preface

I was twenty when I first read *Letters to a Young Poet* by Rainer Maria Rilke. In that book I learned some truths I have never forgotten, about myself and about poetry. Thanks to the truth spoken by those letters and the truths they helped me find, my vocation and path as a poet were never in danger, even at the most difficult moments.

Rilke helped me pose the basic questions and showed me that in poetry to doubt is really to deny, and that, as in so many other aspects of life, to want always to be right is to live in fear you will be proven wrong. I've said that I "learned" these things, but to learn isn't the same as to comprehend. To comprehend means to spend a long time understanding, long enough so that what has been understood is no longer outside us, but forms part of our character. Comprehension is understanding that will never leave us.

I don't know how long it took me to comprehend Rilke's *Letters*, but I know that they were a secure refuge, and were already a part of me, when I was crossing my own poetic desert. I still have my copy, underlined, with notes in the margins, from 1957, by Ediciones Siglo Veinte, Buenos Aires, and it always warms my heart to turn the pages.

I think we know what we are talking about when we say the word *poet* or the word *poetry*, but I would like to clarify that in the pages which follow I never refer to the places where poetry borders on the plastic arts or on music (visual poetry, performance, visual action, etc.). I'm not talking about poetry qualified by adjectives or poetry that is in itself an adjective, but about poems which end up in writing, published and read: poetry as noun, as substantive.

There's another matter I must clarify: the sort of poetry I'm referring to (and to me, this would also be true for the other arts) is based on emotion. What I mean is that I'm not interested in the poem that doesn't help make me a better person, bring about greater inner balance, console me, or leave me a little closer to happiness, whatever it means to be happy.

Poetry can't be defined in terms of rhyme, rhythm or meter, and less still by devaluing those things. I don't believe in art without effort, or believe one needs only to exert oneself in order to write a good poem. Even someone who has read very little—perhaps no more than newspapers and magazines—can become a good reader of poetry. But this doesn't mean that reading a good poem requires no more effort and attention than reading the newspaper. As in all important aspects of life, in poetry nothing comes for free.

New Letters to a

Young Poet

1

Beginning to
Write, Beginning to Publish

I'm addressing someone who has never written to me. Someone I suppose never will. I don't know if anyone other than Mr. Kappus ever wrote Rilke asking about the quality of his poems. But the answer wouldn't have come quickly. In the early years of the twentieth century correspondence was a more leisurely affair, without the haste that often leads people to the mistaken belief that they are poets.

An important difference between our age and the time when Rilke was writing the *Letters to a Young Poet* is how easy it is today to publish a book. There are also countless literary prizes, which serve as a kind of poetic credentialing. One of the chief results of this situation is that the art of poetry is no longer a poor art; it has become one of the merits and useful adornments that can help one climb to a new social or professional level. Naturally, I'm not trying to say the opposite—that whoever has attained a certain professional or social standing cannot be a poet (we need only think of classical Chinese poetry, as an ancient example). What I *am* saying is that poetry is marginal to those things.

If the Rilke of 1903 (though he wasn't very well known yet) were alive today he would surely receive, instead of letters, published books with fervent dedications, and it would be hard for him to distinguish between requests for advice and orientation and mere opportunism, or know whether he was in contact with a beginning poet or merely with one who, more than advice, is seeking approval and even admiration that might prove useful to him in some pursuit unrelated to poetry.

The authentic poet, no matter how young he is, may be uncertain about where he is in his apprenticeship, but he knows perfectly well that he is a poet, and will never question that. Rilke's correspondent, Mr. Kappus, surely wasn't a poet; he was more like the young men who have a book and a literary prize but not the destiny of poets. One can even read the *Letters to a Young Poet* as if they were a work of fiction. Why do I find it so hard to imagine a poet asking if what he writes is poetry? I suppose it's because I believe poetry, in the sense it has been understood for generations, including my own, isn't a trade or a profession but something you decide from within yourself, with scarce possibilities of anyone guaranteeing the rightness of that decision. There is a widespread, dangerous misunderstanding that confuses the well-known phrase "poetry for everyone" with the thought that anyone can write a good poem.

Writing poetry is an operation which tries to bring together in a single flash—the poem—sensations, feelings, the experience of feelings, and intuitions. All this comes together into a reflection of truth. But initially that flash can take place only in the mind of the poet, and the poet must separate feeling from the experience of feeling. It is the experience, not the feeling itself, that leads to the poem. Afterward, so that the flash can be repeated in the mind of the reader, it has to be translated into words, and this must be done without it losing its concision, exactness and intensity. To start this operation, to have the poem *in mente*, you have to be a poet, with certain inborn qualities. Thereafter, as the poem is transformed into words, you need a personal technique, and this too is acquired not externally but by knowing your own inner paths as a developing poet; paths which will teach you to recognize which part of the discovery was made by previous writers and which part is emerging as your own work and isn't found in the poems of other poets. During this process you, as poet, will have to master tools within reach of every apprentice: grammar, syntax, spelling, metrics, rhetoric, and the reading of the classics.

The first proof that the writing of poetry— at least its most important aspects—isn't a trade or a profession is that the poet has to draw on innate qualities. As Heidegger would say, to be a poet is a way of being in the world. A trade or a profession doesn't have to spring from any such innate qualities. It is always better to have natural ability, but even without it, you can understand your profession or trade, and exercise it adequately, so long as you have the appropriate apprenticeship and certain qualities: prudence, constancy, intelligence, and so forth. And there is still another important difference. There are infinite degrees to the efficiency with which people practice their trade or profession, but this isn't the case with poetry. A poem is either a good one or it is nothing, and this is why it can be cruel to have mistakenly believed yourself a poet as a young man or woman, and to have persisted in that erroneous belief through an entire lifetime. Luckily, these things are relatively easy to find out and verify, as Mr. Kappus must have discovered. We can be fooled, sometimes, by factors alien to poetry: ambition, pride, the belief that being known as a poet will help bring us some sort of promotion or advantage. It is also common to take failure in poetry as a sign of the world's injustice. People are always good at manipulating their identity, although it always turns against them, above all, when they write a poem.

So, then... the person I'm addressing is someone who has never asked me whether he or she might become a poet, and who has no doubt he will become one, or is one already; someone who hasn't quite yet found her own poetic voice, but knows it is out there, someplace in the future. And the first thing I would say is that the rush to publish usually leads to future regrets. I remember having asked help from Camilo José Cela when I was a young man. Obligingly, he wrote the prologue to my first book. Today, I prefer that nobody read that book, in which I was still searching for something alien to poetry. I could even say that I hate that book, and the poet I was when I wrote it, and that I feel no fondness for that period in my life. Though it was more difficult, I get along much better with my childhood than with my youth. Once, when the peseta was still in circulation, I found a copy of that first book in a second-hand bookstore. The bookseller asked me for three thousand pesetas and looked at me expectantly, ready to bargain. But both of us knew the book wasn't worth it. I had written it in 1960–61 at the age of 22 or 23, when I was totally devoted to the poetry of Neruda, and I hadn't yet learned that it isn't enough to immerse yourself in the world of the masters: you must also know how to leave it.

I shouldn't have published that book of poems. Its publisher was Pere Vicens, and I've never ceased to feel grateful for his confidence in me. But it wasn't until 1975, when I was 37 and Joaquim Marco published my book of poems, *Crónica,* in Ocnos, his mythical collection, that I first recognized a voice finally my own. This is the book where I now think my poetic work begins. Luckily, after that first book, I learned, or reaffirmed, in Rilke's *Letters to a Young Poet,* all the basics of what I then needed to know.

Necessity

I'm writing these lines in a hotel in the early hours. From the bed I can hear metallic sounds and wood against wood, and, somewhere out there, the beeping that a bulldozer or dump truck make when they are backing up. "Construction," I think. It is the hour of construction projects, the noise of heavy lumber, the clang of steel plates, of workers shouting up and down from different levels of a structure which the crane, like a mother, is helping lift to its feet. This has always been the best time for me to visit a site. I am an architect, and the part of architecture that has always interested me most, more than the planning that goes on in the studio, is the act of construction itself. In fact, for me the basic thing is the gritty work of construction—all that is noisy, ugly, tired, violent. And it's the same for poetry, which arises out of life with its dirt and noise and ugliness. Only when we write from life, and live it fully, can the poem come into existence. It is the one thing that guarantees peace: this initial phase of the work, when we still have no idea what it will finally become.

From the moment the bulldozer lifts its first shovel full of earth or the pickaxes and wrecking ball begin to knock down an old building, still a building, but a dead one, occupying the place where the new construction will be... from that moment on, intensity is everything. There are no noises, no troubles or grit, only construction. There are people who can't accept this, and who look for greater concentration, cleanliness, some way to get quickly to a higher level. It's the same with a musician who can't stand the continual rehearsals, the traveling, the unpleasant venues, the sometimes boring, even abominable contact with other musicians. This is a sign he's about to give up. To write a poem no conditions are better than others, there's only the need to search, find, write, rewrite, work on it until it's done. If a poem can wait, it means that it hasn't found anyone to write it. Not only that—if you want to be a poet and don't know how to convert any personal situation—no matter how difficult—into a situation where your work can continue, you are on the wrong path. If you can't give poetry everything you have—and "everything" means all the truth there is in your life—you shouldn't go on with it.

In his first letter Rilke says we cannot really speak of works of art, "those mysterious existences whose life endures beside our own small, transitory life." I think that the word *mystery* has withdrawn from the work of art, above all from the plastic arts, which have been seeking greater prestige in fleeting and ephemeral ways. We see this reflected in terms like "installation art," "*arte povera*," "minimalism," etc. Not that poetry has been harmed by this. People have gone on writing poetry and no one has been able to write a single good poem that drifted away from the meaning of mystery. Because of this, there is sometimes little opportunity for analysis and criticism: the poem says precisely that which cannot be said in a language which is not, itself, a work of art.

The first thing to determine is whether the thing before you is a poem or not. And this is what Rilke doesn't want to do, although he ends up telling his correspondent, in a very nice way, that his texts are not yet poems. I suppose he avoids Kappus's question because a true poet is infinitely reluctant to waste his time on bad poems, partly because they are useless and partly because he has a vague sense of contamination. It will always be difficult to please someone who writes a bad poem and asks whether it is a poem. We can either lie to him or deal with his ambition, an unpleasant, perfectly futile business. What Rilke does, then, is to set aside Mr. Kappus's poems and write about the paths where one seeks the poem.

What matters most is to know how badly the poet wants to write a poem. Rilke rightly suggests that Kappus ask himself "whether you would have to die if you were forbidden to write," and the question is still valid. I don't think any of the people who say they "don't have time for anything" have ever really passed up whatever it is they wanted with their whole heart, whether it was a date or an important professional opportunity, due to a lack of time. And that's what poetry involves: an imperious, implacable need. If there's no such need, it is useless to try to be a poet. If you take up poetry in a lukewarm way, the relationship will be a bad one and embitter your life without giving you the treasure: the obsession, the passion for poems, the feeling that life doesn't make sense without poetry.

Only when he has this obsession will the poet love problems more than their possible solutions, for poetry arises not from solutions but from problems, and the way to get to the deepest things in life is through what is still unresolved, alive, painfully open. Complaints of any sort are useless, no matter whether they are justified. I would say they are even more useless if justified. Poetry wants nothing to do with sterile complaint. If you have the gift for seeking, finding, and writing a poem, what sense does it make to complain? When you do so, you are confusing the gravity of life, of suffering, its weight within us, with more banal matters of justice or morality. This isn't a matter of romantic exaltation; it's a matter of having enough strength for the poem to come into being. Complain, and you are lacking that strength, which must be felt both by poet and reader. The reader who has "no time to read," who "can never find the right moment," is just as far from that strength and that need as the poet; maybe farther. For to be a good reader is more difficult than to be a bad poet.

Inspiration

Talk about poetry is always a bit disappointing. Professors of literature, if they are good readers of poetry (which sometimes happens), often feel uneasy when they spin a web of erudition around a poem about which, logically speaking, there is very little to say.

What does poetry speak about? If the reader isn't very experienced, I would say that his first reading is usually almost prosaic: it doesn't matter what the poem is speaking about. But on the second reading—which coincides in good readers with the first—the poem pulls the reader onto its own terrain. No one knows how this happens or why it occurs with one specific series of words and not with another. You have to be alone to reach this place, because it is where we find a reflection of our own truth and sometimes a shadow of the world's truth.

Poetry doesn't speak about just anything. Far from it. In any given poem, poetry has spoken of very few things indeed. There isn't time in life for much more. To discover those things and feel the lightning bolt of their reality, the poet has to look at them, analyze them, turn his back on them, turn suddenly around to surprise them, and do this often, countless times, from every possible angle. Since in poetry, as in everything important in life, form and matter are indissolubly joined, every new position that is taken, every new point of view affects both form and matter, and means beginning to look again.

The poet doesn't talk about what he wants to talk about, but what he can and must say— what he *needs* to say—and he usually spends half his life looking for it. This would be a good way to define the poetic apprenticeship, which often begins by pointing out all that it does *not* wish to say. This isn't a bad way to begin, but it risks being too easy. It's always easier to negate than to affirm. Negation leaves us with the false satisfaction of finished work while affirmation is always the threshold of something much more difficult. This is the reproach Elizabeth Bishop leveled at the English poets of the fifties and sixties: "Even Larkin's poetry is a bit too easily resigned to grimness, don't you think? Oh I am all for grimness and horrors of every sort—but you can't have them, either, by shortcuts—by just saying it." This is why when young or unrecognized poets pass harsh—sometimes ferocious—judgment on the poets of the preceding generation, they are wasting their time on useless therapy. I remember the Gregory Peck movie where an old, tired gunfighter comes home to hang up his gun, and there's always a young gunslinger who wants to make history by killing him. And one of them does, shooting him in the back! How much better to create from admiration (the nucleus both of love and of creation) than from rejection!

Whoever writes good poetry knows himself or herself thoroughly—knows his or her inner paths and how to travel them. You can enter those paths from inside or from outside. Any stimulus—a voice, the color of the sky, a memory—carries thought to a specific inner place, and from there it starts down its paths, like the tunnels of a mine, until it finds something special, shining in the dark, and the poet knows that a poem begins there.

But sometimes the poet wanders off course. He can only go through part of that labyrinth with good results. Taking other paths is totally useless: when he does, he produces only a simulated poem. Sometimes he fails to realize he is deceiving himself; that what seem like poems to him, really aren't. That will become clear with time and with other readers, who travel the same paths, only in reverse. If the poem is truly a poem it takes the reader directly to a place inside himself, and there something like a beacon goes on, which is to say that the poet's own deep, difficult inner places greatly resemble those of the reader.

This is why poetry can be written and why it is difficult for a reader of poetry to thumb through a book of poems in a bookstore, read some of them, and not know for sure whether the book is going to interest him or not.

"How poetic!" someone exclaims in the light of a full moon, uttering the words with approval and pleasure. But a full moon isn't yet poetry; in fact, it is still far from poetry. At the origin of a poem there is a *something*, a poetic material that is still totally alien to the word. I agree that these types of impressions are revealing: they are, so to speak, "promises of poems," and when those elements crystallize inside the poet, non-poetry turns into poetry, and the poem adds its own value to that of the *clair de lune*. Nothing of what life and nature offer spontaneously is poetry. But, inside the poet, anything can serve as a point of departure for a poem.

Once the external world has come inside, that world has nothing to offer the poem. Only when the outside is inside us can it start to become material for the poem. But again, this is only a beginning, because the outside world enters into everyone and not only into poets, and within each of us is that same labyrinth of paths, of which few are taken, often the same ones. I don't know what it is that closes off others. Fear? Hate (which is also fear)? Avarice (still another kind of fear)? Perhaps we are simply born with certain paths open and others closed.

In a way we are dealing with the *Nosce te ipsum* of Socrates, more complicated in the case of the poet because we have to add to "Know thyself!" the advice "...and find within yourself the roads that lead to the poem." This is why the enemies of poetry are a sort of ambition, pride, unreality, a certain childishness. They are enemies not from the moral point of view—an important distinction—but from a point of view we could call technical. As Rilke says, at the hour of writing poetry, once some aspect of outer reality has been brought within, or any aspect of one's own world of feelings, it can only disturb the poet deeply to expect any sort of answer from the outside world.

By the end of this process, the poet has merely come to the conclusion that he has to write the poem. This is what is traditionally called inspiration, a complex mixture of intuition and vague guesses about theme and about the direction of the search. Nothing yet of language. The step from here to the poem is another adventure.

Reading a Good Poem

To ask what use is poetry is to ask two questions at once: what use is it to the reader and what use to the writer. But the answer is the same for both. The poet needs to write poetry for the same reason the reader needs to read it, and the triad *Poet—Poem—Reader* is what defines it. If one of the three is missing, poetry doesn't exist.

The poem is a sort of musical score open to many possible interpretations. If it is closed to all but one, it will be perused and quickly forgotten. Continuing with the musical metaphor, the reader isn't the equivalent of the person who listens to a concert, but the musician who interprets the score. The reader's instrument is his sensibility, his culture, feelings, state of mind, frustrations, fears, past history... all this produces an instrument rich in nuances and possibilities. The reader interprets the poem differently each time, and no two people will ever produce the same reading of a poem.

Just as I don't consider the composer more valuable than the interpreter, I don't think a good poet is any more valuable than a good reader. Poetry doesn't happen unless the two of them are drawn irrevocably together. There's no equivalent in poetry of listening to a piece of music. The poem is either interpreted by the reader or it isn't. The intermediary has been eliminated, and there is no one between poem and reader.

In this sense, a poetry recital isn't a true reading; it's merely an approximation, which, for that very reason, usually attracts a very small audience. It may offer, for those who know the poems, the possibility of an interpretation different from their own—above all if it is the poet himself doing the interpretation—and for those who do not know the poems, a sampling, like a movie preview. For those little accustomed to reading poetry, it may simply be a first approach to the genre. But the central poetic fact will always be the interpretation of the poem in the most solitary and intense sort of concert.

And to me this explains the fact that there can be no relaxing of attention during the reading of a poem, as can happen when we read prose or attend a concert. It also explains why readers of novels outnumber those of poetry: the tension of reading a book of poems is necessarily greater. Even with good novels, the novelist deliberately relaxes the tension of reading, that's part of his literary technique. He does so to make the story work. Even good, demanding novels have readers that enter them expecting to be entertained. Good poetry doesn't allow that sort of reading.

It may seem paradoxical that, on the one hand, a book of poems should demand the maximum tension from the reader and, on the other, not require any special preparation. But there is no contradiction; it's only that people lack trust in one another. We believe we are more dissimilar than we really are. Faced with the harshness of life, we are all very similar. When someone we love dies, we feel the same thing whether we're powerful or powerless. What makes us different from one another is simply our ability to explain an event. But what happens to us also happens, or can happen, to everyone else. As I said when discussing inspiration, this is precisely the reason poetry can be written.

The comparison between poetry and music brings out a number of other revealing similarities. For example, one thing that matters in a poem is dissonance: something not yet resolved, a hint left to the reader to interpret. A poem, like a musical piece, is a series of dynamic effects which converge on a resting point where different meanings seem to come together. The melody would be the poetic element that creates intensity in the reader, and it is the very most difficult thing to teach someone if he lacks the innate gift to be a composer or poet.

The person who reads a poem well interprets it with an instrument so precisely in tune that no one can play it better than that reader. In order to play it, the only preparation required is a sense of need and the decision to do so. Any sort of life can make us master that instrument. Even someone in the most miserable cultural circumstances can derive some advantage from a good poem. All sorts of difficult times—wars, revolutions (I think of the Russian gulags)—have shown this to be true.

5

Understanding a Good Poem

For centuries poetry distinguished itself from prose by its formal characteristics, above all rhyme and meter. These differences have grown less significant and today what distinguishes poetry from prose are concision and exactness. Regarding concision, I would say that a poem has the structure of a building with exactly the right beams and pillars: were we to eliminate even one, the building would come tumbling down. If a single word is eliminated from a poem, or replaced by another, and nothing important happens, it wasn't really a poem. Or it wasn't yet a poem. It only becomes one when you cannot eliminate, add, or change any piece of the structure. But this doesn't necessarily make it a good poem. Quality is tied more closely to another characteristic: exactness. Exactness means that a poem must say just what the future reader needs, most of the time without the reader knowing he needs it. And naturally, the poet does not know this future reader. Obviously, such a complex operation must fail most of the time.

Mathematics are the most exact of the sciences, and poetry, the most exact branch of letters. Thanks to this exactness, poetry can console us. Poetry can come into our solitude and produce a change, a greater inner order amid the continuous outer disorder of life. Sometimes we use entertainment to calm our anxiety over this disorder, but the difference between that and reading a poem is that we emerge from entertainment the same way we entered; we've merely passed the time. But when we are done reading a good poem we are no longer the same; our sense of inner order has been enhanced.

What should poetry be like? I would say that a poem must be able to be understood. No one should tell a person who has been reading for years—reading whatever: poetry, novel, essay, the press—that he cannot understand a poem because poetry is difficult. This problem barely existed until the rise of the Avant-Gardes, which proposed to break not only with the past but also with what was, at the beginning of the twentieth century, the present. Painting filled with faces and landscapes with no model in reality, and literature, with texts that seemed to be written in unknown languages and grammars. But in fact, the main goal of those artists was to show they had broken with the acting and thinking typical of the society of their day. This was the very first large-scale advertising campaign; the very invention of advertising. Art enriched itself with the discovery of new forms of expression and poets applied them immediately to their own work. A new sort of poetry was now possible: one which might say nothing at all, but (according to the postulates of the period) was supposed to show a revolutionary attitude. Much time has gone by since then, and, although all of those causes and effects seem remote from us, there are still poets and intellectuals who, when people find a poem unintelligible, say that they lack the training or sensitivity to understand it. This is a field where people often give undue importance to things that are scarcely real; even philosophers have done so, and the seriousness of the questions they pose doesn't always save them from a lack of good sense. This absurd attitude, new in the history of poetry, has discouraged readers in a ritual self-destruction that seems to aspire to a poetry that says nothing and is read by no one.

To me, the only valid poetry is poetry that is understood. But what do we mean by "understood"? As I said earlier, those who have read a good poem have the sense that they are no longer the same people they were before reading it. It is this feeling that shows the poem has been *understood*. It means that the reader is ready to think about the poem and continue reading and interpreting it without the need for some special gift or some special enabling circumstance. Almost every time that a poem seems an impenetrable bunker, it is the poet's fault.

It's one thing to say that the poem doesn't place too many previous demands on its readers, and quite another to say that writing or reading poetry is a naive and simple-minded activity: there is nothing farther from ingenuous spontaneity than poetry. Poetry is the final limit we are permitted to reach participating in life and things.

A good poem is probably, most of all, a matter of intensity. And what we associate with intensity is the experience of feeling, whether the feeling is hidden or obvious. Wherever there is intensity, poetry can exist. This is why poetry has to be exact and concise. Intensity means concentration. But this doesn't mean that the poem doesn't have to be understood. On the contrary! Again, what do we mean by "understanding"? Gabriel Ferrater was cheating when he said we must be able to understand a poem the way we understand a business letter. It's a brilliant dictum, and we all know what he means, but understanding the poem is a more complex process. I take that process, and the "understanding" of poetry, to involve an entrance and an exit and what information theory calls a black box. Input goes into the box and comes out altered, without our knowing what happened inside. And thus with the poem: someone enters the poem in a certain inner state—what I would call (to use another term from information theory) a degree of "disorder" caused by fear, sadness, loss, and all that constantly threatens our inner harmony. If the disorder is less when that person exits the poem, it means that it was a good poem and that it has been understood.

There aren't many black boxes that alter our solitude and leave it feeling consoled, happier, with a keener sense of order. Poetry's powers might be limited, but without them we would find it harder to brave the elements of life. In this sense, as I've said in a poem, poetry is our ultimate refuge, our orphanage, our House of Mercy.

6
Poetry and Literature

The word literature means all that has been written and the place it is kept. But today it is also used in a more restrictive sense to single out novels, and exclude other genres, especially books of science and technology. This slippage of meaning responds to the way humans have modified and transformed reality. There has been a growing specialization, most evidently of knowledge but also, and this is what matters to us, of attitudes toward the written word. More than ever, the good reader knows what he is looking for. It has been a long time since readers defined their interests in general terms like knowledge and entertainment. In view of this specialized sense of "literature," I would say that making a poem has less to do with literature than it might seem. And yet, on the other hand, it makes no sense to try to write "original" poetry, directly and rapidly, by not reading poetry. A young man who aspires to be a poet once told me that he didn't read "so as not to be contaminated"!

What people choose to read, and how they shape their interests, is, of course, a question of attitude: we read what we need, and our needs are modified by our reading. The poet's reading needs can be too eclectic to describe, or prescribe. What we know is that those readings will help him search for the difficult, inner pathways where the poem is generated. For example, I got an unforgettable sense of the truth a good poem should transmit when I read Galileo's argument against Aristotle, who had said mistakenly that bodies fall faster the heavier they are. It may be— it was my own case— that *Darwin's Voyages* or a good book of cosmology can contribute more to a poet's education (I think gratefully of The *Nature of the Physical World* by Sir Arthur S. Eddington) than great works of literature like *Don Quixote* or Joyce's *Ulysses*. And one can feel more indebted to Du Fu or a poem by Mayakovski than to Jorge Guillén or Carles Riba.

According to Coromines, *literature* comes from the Latin *litteratura*, which was the translation of the Greek *tekné grammatiké*, the art of reading and writing. But the word *poet* comes from the Greek *poietés*, maker or creator. At a certain moment (we see an echo of this in Plato) writing was an innovation that conflicted with the deep sense of *poietés*. Writers and grammarians are a foretaste of those who, many centuries later, would be known as intellectuals, and from Plato's time on, intellectuals have always had a difficult relationship with poetry because there is a certain primitivism, a certain austerity in the poet (even more radical in the world of music) and a reluctance to engage in disquisitions about literature. We might say that the relationship between poetry and literature is similar to the one between mysticism and religion, without this meaning that poetry has anything to do with mysticism or literature with religion. Poetry needs to concentrate on the sparest, driest, deepest part of the real world, but that concentration vanishes or gets dispersed in the labor of classification and interpretation that reality demands of the intellectual. At least this is the feeling we sometimes have when writing poetry. There have always been other factors to deepen the conflict—really a conflict of interest—between intellectuals and poets. You can't be an intellectual or a critic without authors and works to discuss and it isn't uncommon to see an intellectual tangle the poem in affirmations and negations and set himself up as unavoidable middleman between the poem and the public; that is, the people for whom poems are written. This sort of power grab involves money, prestige, or mere vanity, in the case of intellectuals who would like to turn themselves into creators, an attempt almost always pathetic and useless. There is no one less qualified to speak of poetry than the person who has tried to be a poet and, on failing, turns to criticism. No true poet can expect anything good from that sort of game.

To write good poetry you must read the sort of good novels that leave the sediment, the background against which we can glimpse the initial outline of a poem. We will never know how a given novel has been useful to specific poetic moments or poems, but we do know that many modern poems would be much worse, or wouldn't exist at all, without a certain number of good novels. Some good novels hold more meaning for the poet than others. In the process of writing a poem, they play a role similar to that of classical poetry. They come to bear directly on individual poems, and at times on entire books, in a way that maybe more evident to the poet himself than to others. Again, it's hard to identify specific novels or characteristics—they vary from poet to poet—but to me it is evident that the delicate works of Jens Peter Jacobsen recommended by Rilke—*Niels Lyhne* and *Marie Grubbe*—belong to this category. I would add works as different as *The Magic Mountain* by Thomas Mann, the *Alexandria Quartet* by Lawrence Durrell, *Life and Fate* by Vasily Grossman, *The Heart is a Lonely Hunter* by Carson McCullers, *Sabbath's Theater* by Philip Roth, *Anna Karenina* by Lev Tolstoy, all of the work of Richard Yates, and the stories of Hemingway, Rodoreda, Carver, Aldecoa, Cheever and Salter.

Poetry and Tradition

One of the most important parts of the young poet's apprenticeship is reading the classics of poetry, the unforgettable poets whose work has retained strength and interest despite the passage of time.

The work of a classical poet is always full of suggestions for one's own work and reading the classics is a constant poetic "cure," offering hope and indispensable inner peace, even for the poet who is most *maudit*, and who is writing a good poem. For the same reason, we shouldn't waste time on bad poetry. A bad poem is never an innocent act, and isn't even useful as an experience. This is another proof that poetry is not a profession; in it, errors do not teach or enrich us; they give us nothing. From my master, the architect José Antonio Coderch, I learned to reject the seduction of the word *originality*, one of the most dangerous for a poet. Speaking of architecture, Coderch used to say that a house needn't be "independent or original or sumptuous or made in vain." It occurs to me now that he could have been speaking about any human activity, especially poetry. All the good poetry ever written is, for me, a huge frieze where the poets of the past have left their mark. Whoever writes a good poem does the same. To emphasize the novelty or originality of that mark doesn't really seem a worthwhile pursuit.

But we also need a certain frankness, a certain lack of inhibition when we write a poem, and we can't allow ourselves to be overwhelmed by the past. *What can I say after Baudelaire, Horace, or Hardy?* is a question that can abort any possibility of writing, depending on how it is formulated. An excellent poet and good friend of mine fell victim to that sort of daunting inhibition—Segimon Serrallonga, who was sometimes paralyzed by thinking of his master Carles Riba. This is one of the principal contradictions of poets. They need to be bold with respect to the past, but that boldness is worth nothing if they don't also feel humility—the humility felt by all great poets. You have to be bold when writing the poem and humble before and after. A second contradiction is that, although the poet usually shows a certain tendency to solitude and this implies a certain disdain for others, he needs their recognition, sometimes with a shameful intensity; for without readers the poem does not exist.

The first contradiction is a healthy one: only mediocrity doesn't know how to manage the interplay of humility and boldness. The mediocre poet often turns them into pride and ignorance, a mix which produces the worst poems imaginable. The second contradiction is a residue of Romanticism and is one of the difficulties young poets face today as they modulate their own voices. I'm referring to the need to situate their work in relation to the past, and in particular to the two artistic and literary movements that still exert the most influence: Romanticism and the movements of the Avant-Garde.

The principal feature of Romanticism, perhaps the only one common to its many variants, is the rejection of the classical canons and, by extension, of any overly structured set of rules. The rejection is made in the name of spiritual freedom, the affirmation of irrationality and the poetic transfiguration of reality. These concepts re-emerge later in all sorts of Avant-Garde manifestos, most of which now seem rather puerile. And yet, one thing is what artists say and another what they do. Romantic poetry, painting and music were always formally impeccable and respected the rules, even the classical ones. The most unrestrained poetry of Romanticism was never very transgressive, at least not formally; it was in the realm of content, not form, where it posed its challenges.

But Romanticism posed an issue that is still very important today: the identification of poetry with life. Romanticism tried to adapt life to a certain "Romantic" attitude. It demanded that life look at itself in the mirror of Romantic poetry and literature, and it gave new value to the extraordinary. The movements of the Avant-Garde made the Romantic postulates fully their own, in both form and content, and reality was totally transfigured. Once again it became a basic premise to adapt life to poetry, and not poetry to life. In a lecture about Rilke given between the wars, Stefan Zweig complains that it is difficult to find a pure poet, and, even more difficult, a purely poetic existence, a life perfectly adjusted to poetry. Back then, one lived in the midst of the most exalted Romantic vision. Rilke lived the way he was able to, or wanted to, surely a little of both, but what matters isn't how Rilke lived but the belief in an essence that exists outside of life—poetry— on which the poet, when he reaches this world, must pattern his existence. In this sense, the Avant-Garde movements showed their conservative Christian legacy, which believes continually in the future as the only way to confront a past which it cannot or does not wish to understand.

As for me, I like to think that I write from what I call an intelligence of feeling, which distrusts the absence of rules and which, instead of refusing them, embraces all sorts of formal possibilities, denying participation only to irrationality. In poetry this means that any rule can be acceptable, any canon, from seamless classicism to the use of the meters of the Middle Ages and Renaissance to the introduction of free verse, and the disappearance of the known metrical structures, leaving an indeterminate border between poetry and prose. With respect to reality, this sort of intelligence goes in the opposite direction from Romantic and Avant-Garde transfiguration. It starts from reality and reveals the poems contained in reality. Put differently, it adapts poetry to reality, that is to life. The tool this "intelligence of feeling" uses to open the way from the most immediate into the deepest reality is the experience of emotion, which is always governed by reason, and even more closely by common sense. I can't think of a single great poem that contains anything senseless.

Poetry has no end because reality too is endless. Each poet, if he finds his own voice, will be able to bring out a different nuance of this reality and the nuances and poetic voice will always sound new. There is no good poem which does not somehow include the poems of the past with their artistic substances, some ancient, some nearer to us, and their expression of pain, death, love, evil, happiness, fear, and guilt. Each generation reinterprets these concepts, feelings, experiences and thoughts, just as each generation must retranslate the great works of literature written in other languages because to translate them is to reinterpret them, and get them ready to be read anew by those who follow.

Speaking of translation, I believe it is one of the most intense ways to draw close to poetry written in another language. In contrast to the old adages that the *traddutore* is a *traditore*, and that poetry is precisely what is lost in translation, a good poem usually survives translation, and the translation, no matter how bad, cannot fail to reveal that the original is good. In general,

I prefer for the translated poem to *say* the same as it does in the original. But a poem *says* from many perspectives, it is a polyhedron with many facets and reflections and it is this multiplicity of readings that gives rise to the necessary sacrifices (not acts of treason) of the translator. I also prefer to search for expressiveness in concision and in internal rhythms which are often not very apparent, rather than in the rhyme or stanza forms of the original. After all, rhyme has a different meaning in different languages. In Catalan or in English, for example, it is less blunt and forceful than it sometimes is in Castilian, where, when it appears, it strongly affects the poem. But I have seen magnificent translations done with totally contrary criteria; that is, those which take formal elements—rhyme and meter, for example—as the ones to be retained in the translation All these questions must be posed without dogmatism; all that matters in poetry are the results.

When dealing with poems of the past, the translator has to decide if he is going to do a historical reading or a contemporary one. This is important, for depending on which aspects of the poem are emphasized, translation of the same original can lead to very different poems. I don't believe we can ever speak of *the* translation of a poem. To translate is to show a poem from different angles, leaving it invisible from many others and only half visible from most. There is no "treason" whatsoever if one states from the outset from what angles the translation has been made. Each epoch should renew its translations, along with its points of view.

A special case, but of smaller proportions, is bilingualism. I am a bilingual poet, and the bilingual editions of my books don't exactly have Catalan poems translated into Castilian; rather the poems are written almost at the same time in both languages. This is the result of the linguistic, political, and geographic circumstances of many like me who were born into Catalan families during the Civil War or its aftermath. The poet can have one or many cultural languages, but none of them gets him to the place where the poem is. As in a fairy tale, you have to enter a secret crypt and know the password. This doesn't apply when your mother tongue is the same as your cultural language. When it is not, the cultural language can be a cathedral built on a crypt and you can only go down to and enter that crypt through the mother tongue. I reach that place in Catalan and immediately set up the framework of the poem in Catalan. Usually, I work it through, and the final version bears little resemblance to the initial one. I produce the successive versions and modifications at the same time in Catalan and in Castilian, but it is only in my mother tongue that I can get the poem started.

One way or another, the writing of the poem has to follow a certain order, based on rational rules. To write poetry, it isn't useful, most of the time, to liberate feeling from the control of reason. As Voltaire said, "When I write *I am crying*, I don't need to cry." Nor must we pretend to be original. In general terms I agree with Thomas Hardy when he says that "All we can do is to write on the old themes in the old styles, but try to do a little better than those who went before us." I would qualify that by saying we exist as poets thanks to what previous poets did in different traditions, and that in the best of cases we will add a modest stroke of our own to this frieze, which is the history of poetry.

It doesn't seem that there can be an apprenticeship to poetry that is distant from the great poets who went before us, because the poetic apprenticeship has this in common with all learning practices: you begin by copying, by trying to acquire a knowledge of all that is important and has already been written. You imitate and read the great poets, their complete works if possible, reading from the latest toward the earliest, because it is in the poems of youth where we are least likely to find things worth learning.

It is good practice to copy out by hand the poems which seem most interesting. After that, without looking at them, you can try to write the poem you've just copied. A little later, try to address the same theme or a very similar one and write a poem imitating the manner and style of the poem copied earlier. This series of exercises allows us to probe a little more deeply into the chosen poem, and to re-read the original in another way. And never forget for a moment the basic tools for writing poetry: grammar, meter, and rhetoric. Nothing could be more mistaken than to opt out of this apprenticeship in the name of a supposed modernity that will be no more than a futile apology for ignorance. No one can say, without knowing and using them, that these tools, employed by so many good poets, will be useless. This is the part of the poetic apprenticeship which can be taught. It's a basic part, but this alone isn't enough to write a good poem. In mathematics, this would be called a necessary but not a sufficient condition.

The rest of the apprenticeship, all of it, belongs to the poet and no one else, in his or her solitude, with no guide but the classics to develop his or her capacity for inspiration and self criticism, the two most precious goods in the writing of poetry. This is only the beginning of the poet's work, for a brief moment of inspiration can generate much work later on. And we ought not to make light of any negative criticism, no matter how little we think of the poetic culture of the reader, if it has been made in good faith. We should consider it seriously, as if we had heard it from the most valuable and demanding critic. When a reader, no matter who he is, stumbles in a poem, we should find out what made him do so. That way, we will develop our self-critical powers to the maximum and strike at the useless complacency to which all of us are inclined.

Poetry, Philosophy, and Religion

For the young poet one of the most fearful of traps is the cliché. There are minefields where we need a certain experience and a mature poetic voice. Rilke points to love poems as one of these areas, and I think he was right. Another is religion and philosophy, with the latter sometimes meandering into the terrain of politics. All these fields have a tendency to reverse roles with poetry and use it to their own ends. Philosophy and religion have always been tempted to use poetry to probe people's relationship with myth and with God, the most important of myths.

In a certain type of poetry, religion and metaphysics have always been closely allied.

This is true in Castilian poetry, where there is a tradition of mystical poetry with an emphasis on the transcendent. In Catalan poetry, though much of society has a Catholic substratum, aside from what one can find in past times, above all in Ramon Llull, there hasn't been much worthwhile religious poetry. The poetry of Verdaguer is basic for all Catalan poets—all by itself, it brought back a lost literary language—but it has no importance as religious poetry. Verdaguer is a contemporary of Hopkins, but the two aren't really comparable. Hopkins has all of English poetic tradition behind him, and Verdaguer, an abyss. Personally, I find Catholic religious poetry unconvincing. This is what I feel with some of the Polish poets: Milosz, for example, was a great poet, and had a great Catholic poetic sensibility, but when he took that path he wrote some extremely boring poems that are as superficial as the catechism. This is also the case, though less evident, of Vinyoli, who lowers the high level of his poems whenever he uses poetry as a tool for religious or mystical research.

Catholicism (and I'm still talking about *poetry*, not religion) is based on a pact-like relationship between the God of monotheism and his faithful. God threatens and punishes but afterwards pardons, and Catholicism provides every facility for repentance. Original sin is a mere point of departure, easily resolved: it is almost a sort of connivance with the divinity. It is difficult for this to lead to great poetry. Hopkins' case would be an exception or perhaps, poetically speaking, his anguish is more proper to a Protestant poet. Catholicism is born in sensual Mediterranean lands which would never have been able to produce, for example, a Kierkegaard, so close to Hopkins and so distant from Saint John of the Cross. Reading the latter, I can't help feeling that what has been called mystical poetry in our corner of the world is simply the heated imagining of saints. Saint John of the Cross has the magnificent sound of his Castilian—his enormous *soledad sonora*—but he also has a mystical sensuality that, today, I find disquieting and sometimes even repulsive.

It seems to me that mysticism aspires to reach a place beyond that of poetry, outside the world, with a sterile clarity or darkness, a territory which—I confess—makes me share the old suspicion that the mystics are mystifiers, sometimes despite themselves. Poetry tries hard to do the very opposite: help us live life with the least mystification possible, without succumbing to fear; live with the maximum dose of truth that we can stand, which isn't much, because truth, as in Greek tragedies, destroys the person who uncovers it. The poet, too, is a mystic—the rare mystic who is able to *explain* what he has seen. As if words, the names of things, set up a line of defense, a protective barrier, against the terror of the world. Poetry shelters us with those words and allows us to penetrate again, prudently, into the chilling infinity that begins on the other side of language: a place where the mystics, too, have been, without being able to explain what it is they saw.

As for philosophy, I would be ungrateful if I didn't recognize how much it has helped me. I've been helped, most of all, by the classical Greeks, the Pre-Socratics like Parmenides and Heraklitus, who wrote poetry. I've also been helped by the amiable common sense of Montaigne, the raw solitude of Kierkegaard, the difficult clarity of Wittgenstein or the vital voluptuousness, despite its shadows and its insomnia, of Cioran. I think and read philosophy as if it were a desperate pre-sentiment of poetry and of music.

But the philosophers seek arguments that answer to certain, pre-established points of view of their own and for the most part, when they use poetry, they use minor works. What reader today has any patience for the texts by Breton or Aragon that Walter Benjamin considered significant and utilized as paradigms? Benjamin used them to prove that "only the Surrealists have understood the present-day commands" of the *Communist Manifesto.* In reaching conclusions like this, great poems don't help very much. That quote from Benjamin is from 1929, and I shudder to think how many splendid poets and poems he had around him. It is an old operation: drawing on poems or poets who aren't very important, a thinker extracts conclusions that, most of the time, will end up being shown to have little substance. This is the case of the perverse operation Heidegger attempts with a very boring poem by Hölderlin. Or the case of Breton and Benjamin, which I've just mentioned. But it is also thanks to similar operations that poets such as Pessoa or Cavafy, who are good poets, hold an exaggeratedly high place in our esteem. In general, I don't think philosophers have added much to the comprehension of poetry and even less to its enjoyment.

When people give poetry a secondary role in some activity, they almost never choose great poems, because good poetry doesn't allow itself to be manipulated, not even with the best of intentions. The history of music is full of lyrics we listen to and remember almost always because of the composer, without anyone remembering the poet or the poem. Very little music has thrived using great poems as lyrics. Naturally, there are exceptions but they are very few.

The validity of poetry has nothing to do with who is defending it. Anyone can capture it, without special privileges, although at times we can understand a poem but not explain what we've found there or what it makes us feel. This happens even to those who pass as cognoscenti (and hide beneath a certain rhetoric) and it also happens to the poet, whose only explanation of the poem is the poem itself.

When the poet writes, he cannot think about whether the poem will prove useful. Occasional verse doesn't usually constitute an important part of a poet's work. Almost all of the political, so-called social poetry of the 50s and 60s in Spain was occasional verse. I don't think that those who didn't write social poetry under Franco loved freedom any less than people who did. As Miquel Bauçà told me one day in 1964, when Franco was commemorating "25 years of peace" with all the pomp of his regime: "25 years of peace? No, Joan. Maybe 25 years of Marxism." What he meant was that, back then, it was then practically obligatory (we didn't yet have the expression "politically correct") to sit through the boring sermons of young "progressives" who had the same fervent dogmatism as their Catholic parents.

And the semantic content of a poem doesn't have to be transcendent for the poem to be so. There are countless lyrics like this folksong about the two "pilgrims" of Cabra, collected and arranged by García Lorca, a poem which, as I recently discovered, not even the young poets of Cabra still remember:

Hacia Roma caminan dos pelegrinos
a que los case el Papa, mamita,
porque son primos, niña bonita.

Y el Papa les pregunta de dónde eran,
y ella dice de Cabra, mamita,
y él de Antequera, niña bonita.

Y el Papa les pregunta si han pecado,
y ella dice que un beso, mamita,
él le había dado, niña bonita.

Toward Rome go the two pilgrims
to be married by the Pope, *Mamita*,
because they are cousins, *niña bonita*.

And the Pope asks them where they were
                                                        from,
and she says from Cabra, *Mamita*,
and he, from Antequera, *niña bonita*.

And the Pope asks them if they have sinned,
and she says a kiss, *Mamita*,
is what he gave her, *niña bonita*.

Often poems like this one carry us qui-
etly away to some lost personal paradise.
Transcendence occurs the moment we read
these verses and add their sweet, simple music,
and set into motion meanings which the words
didn't know they had: the lyrics are no longer
the same, we no longer see them objectively. In a
good poem like this, there is no optimism or pes-
simism. All good poems nurture life, even those

about death and its environs. But we shouldn't forget that poetry can also be cruel, from the moment it is disposed to reveal some sort of truth.

Poetry and Love

A poetical work is always a rather exact reflection of what love means for the poet, because the poet advances only by deepening the relationship between poetry and love. This is one of the most basic, longest, and most difficult parts of a poet's training.

We feel love for inanimate things when we have turned them into a symbol of what no longer exists and allow the echo of their presence to shelter us in new ways; every symbol is a refuge. And everything related to love partakes of the mystery of repetition. A face must be repeated to be loved, and our eyes return often to the photo that evokes some person or some place we love. There is the repetition of waking up in the same house, or going out onto the same street. Repetition and fear are the foundation of love. It is repetition that turns an object into a symbol (a conversion which never happens overnight) and often it is fear that pushes us toward that comforting repetition. What we call love is the action of turning something into a symbol and seeking protection there. The sensuality and sexuality of the original object must become part of the symbol, and this is a dangerous operation in poetry, for the original intensity can be lost.

The love poem grows more complex the more directly it deals with a peculiar person. Aside from friendship and the love of a couple, social custom classifies love according to family relationships. Love is maternal, paternal, filial, and fraternal. Here too repetition is fundamental, but protection occurs not in a symbolic way but directly, without intermediaries, with each person symbolizing himself, which is poetically more complex. As for the poem that speaks of the love of one person for another, in physical proximity, that sort of poem always feels pressured either toward the exaltation of love or its destruction. These poetic acts of exaltation and destruction can range from the obvious (which is when the poem is most difficult) to the very subtle, in which there is an almost imperceptible change of internal rhythm, so slight that one cannot tell whether the poem is exalting or destroying, or whether it is really a love poem at all.

When we are writing a love poem there is always the danger of something else intruding—some custom, some bit of morality of less poetic interest. When poetry speaks of love, it becomes much more dramatically apparent than it is in other circumstances how hard it is to speak the truth. It also becomes clearer than ever that without truth there is no poem. But what makes the love poem especially complex is the need to know exactly how to reflect the character and the intensity of sex. The poem can treat it explicitly, as a major, unique force, or have it participate like a suggestion impregnating the whole poem. Things are most difficult when the poem enters the realm of a couple defined by their sexual relationship and shows how their refuge or protection is lacking or has been destroyed, or, to the contrary, the poem describes its comforting presence. All this can be posed in more or less idealistic terms and related to a variety of social components—fashion, morals, customs, the past—which pose no threat to good poets but which wreak havoc on mediocre ones.

Love poems are always a refuge and, for this reason, their catastrophic renderings of loss are always more imaginary than real. A love poem can deal with many things: physical intimacy; the way helplessness depends on the little warm places of love (the "place of excrement" of Yeats); the lovers' possessiveness of those places; the rupture of these unbearable equilibriums. Love poems need to understand the relationship between the orgasm—life's deepest mission—and guilt, and understand the mysterious punishment of Onan. Understand why the emptiness after orgasm should fill with words that carry us toward the symbolism of friendship or despair.

In order to write the love poem of a couple we have to understand their struggle with the anxious, ferocious tug of the quotidian, knit together from feelings of security and fear.

To capture all this with the intense, concise, exact word is almost impossible, but it is what makes poetry; it is what Catullus has done, and Petrarch, Propertius and Larkin. The love poem breaks through to the place where each of us keeps his private hell, a place where sex helps mix the poison that brings about the spectacular losses of old age.

Poetry's mission is to use the word to find truth in this thicket of connections (connections repeated, lost, substituted for). It must do so without succumbing to the deceits that cloak themselves in brilliance. You can take a difficult shortcut, like the relationship between love and death, accessible only to the classics (Ausias March, Manrique, Donne, Ronsard, Quevedo, Baudelaire, Hardy, Yeats, Machado, Estellés), or you can deliberately and prudently stay away from that terrain, as Espriu did. One way or the other, no foundations are deeper than those of love and sex, and these are the substrata poetry ought to reach for.

Poems that speak of love for someone who has died require extreme delicacy, prudence, and distance. This is hard because with this sort of poem the poet has no chance to remember from a distance; he must write before the unstoppable process of oblivion wipes out the scene he has imagined and needs for the poem. When oblivion seeps into pain, circumstances have changed and the poem is already something else.

Sex, death, symbol, myth, repetition... all are threatened by the tiredness of daily life. In the love poetry written in one's youth, love is often laced with fear. The more uninhibited the poem seems, the more this is true; this is why Rilke recommends leaving love poems for later. But one mustn't stop thinking about them, reading, seeking the inner paths which lead to them. Love is a crowded city never completely known, with neighborhoods of all sorts, some old or in ruins, some new or still under construction.

There are poverty and wealth, mediocrity, all sorts of diseases, the best music and the worst possible crimes, cold winters and suicidal summers. The sun can shine brightly, the rain can be desolate, and the city looks different depending on the way we look at it. When you emerge from the usual places, the surprises—from ecstasy to horror—are continual, and an entire life is never enough to express even a few of its truths in a few poems.

10

Poetry and Solitude

There are acts that involve a huge number of people making a lot of noise—sporting events, political rallies, demonstrations—and other quieter, more minoritarian ones: concerts (of classical music), movies, poetry recitals. Recitals can take place in the solitude of one's own room, of an airport, a train, the waiting room of a hospital, because today we have access to music and poetry from all these places.

It is in this solitude that poetry reaches its maximum intensity, and this solitude that allows us to deepen our reading of a poem and accept the consolation it offers. It is in solitude that we gain the possibility of not limiting life to sensuality and entertainment, which is a way to ignore ourselves and feel proud of that form of ignorance (a major part of what we might call illiteracy in today's world): the tendency to hollow out life with empty spaces that reverberate with fear.

Poetry isn't the antechamber of solitude, it *is* solitude, and the young poet should know that what he is beginning isn't a path to self realization parallel to some other, more important path he has proposed for himself. This is what people think for whom poetry is a hobby. A poet inspires fear because of the truth he seeks and the solitude he brings. The environment will always try to marginalize him or prevent him, *seriously speaking*, from becoming a poet.

Because poetry is not a profession, the true poet is hard to manipulate. Two principle means of manipulation are family and work. But the pressures of work can be resisted. As for family, it has never, not even in the worst of cases, been able to corrupt a true poet. I don't know what it is we seek in procreation, in sexual relations, but surely it is to form part of the vast design that Rilke wrote about. Within this complexity, males and females may differ more than we like to think, not in areas like intelligence or human rights, but in their attitudes and in the tools they use to brave the material and moral storms of life. In any case, I think that only someone who can traverse this solitude without poetic harm (I won't say suffering), is truly a poet.

To write poetry is an obsession in the good sense of the word, and since the persistent idea that takes hold of the mind is beneficent, having much to do with truth and consolation. This helps protect the poet in his search, but he cannot eliminate contradictory feelings from his immediate surroundings: in the end, everyone wants the thing he fears. If obsessions pull a person away into solitude, the obsession of poetry does this more forcefully, without offering any sort of practical corporate spirit with other poets who live in similar conditions. Friendship among poets demands mutual admiration. One poet cannot be the intimate friend of another who does not value his work.

I would counsel the young poet not to lose too much time in the places where poetry comes into contact with social life. He will discover false poets precisely because they insist on dominating those places. The poet ought to reflect on the reasons for solitude and where it comes from, and think about the role individualism plays in good modern poems, which begin with the character who speaks in *Les Fleurs du mal,* though that individualist isn't so far from that of Achilles in the *Iliad.* The young poet should think that his apprenticeship to poetry is, at the same time, an apprenticeship to solitude. No one has ever matured without going through some inner commotion, loss, or anguish, and good poems show how important it is to have experienced pain. This is why we need poetry, for not even love can be understood without the experience of suffering.

As poets and readers know, this road toward inner growth carries us toward lucidity and truth. It's a matter of facing up to disorder, pain, evil, so that they are illuminated—like the loaf of bread in one of Dalí's best paintings—with a clarity that is a consolation in itself. A clarity which allows us mysteriously to live without the need to forget. To me this is the domain of poetry, and this is the illumination offered by the poem. This is the way both poet and reader can find their own ways to face solitude.

Afterword

One of Joan Margarit's recent poems, published in *Casa de Misericordia* (*House of Mercy*), winner of Spain's National Poetry Award, evokes the years following Spain's Civil War and of his childhood (he was born in 1938); years when food, clothing and adequate shelter were so scarce, and living conditions so bleak, that mothers, even those whose husbands had fought against Franco, overcame their fear, went to the doors of Catholic orphanages, and begged for their children to be admitted. In an epilogue, Margarit explains the genesis of his poem:

I conceived it while visiting an exhibition on the Casa de Misericordia, where I could see photos and documents tied to its history. Three things stuck in my mind. In the first place, the building—huge, austere, shiningly clean, with the boys and girls always serious, whether sitting or standing, in an almost military order. Next, the applications, many of which were from the widows of those assassinated in the period of repression at the end of the Civil War, who were asking for their children to be admitted, since it was impossible to support them. And in the third place, the way the judges and other civil servants responded to those applications. (Tr. Anna Crowe)

The exhibition must have stirred up personal memories—Margarit's own father had been incarcerated after the war—and he took to the exhibition, or took away from it, an important image: that of poetry as refuge, as a "casa de misericordia"—a cruel one at times—to which, in the midst of a spiritual landscape of desolation (death and loss, disease, personal failure, social disorder) man can still have access. "Poetry's powers might be limited," Margarit writes in these pages, "but without them we would find it harder to brave the elements of life. In this sense... poetry is our ultimate refuge, our orphanage, our House of Mercy."

New Letters to a Young Poet (2007) celebrates poetry, its devotion to truth, its cruelty and consolations. It is not a series of letters, like the little book by Rilke (published in 1929) to which it pays homage, but an ardent defense of poetry in which Margarit shares some of the practical wisdom—about poetry and about the rest of life—he has learned from decades of writing poems in Spanish (since the early 1960s) and in Catalan (since 1981) and from reading and translating poetry from English into those two languages (as a devoted translator of poets, from Thomas Hardy to Elizabeth Bishop). This little book is also an apology for clarity and a brief for the poetry which tries to communicate, "exactly and concisely," the emotions and experiences of everyday life. One of the lessons Margarit learned from Rilke is that "poems are not (as people think) feelings, they are experiences," and those experiences are firmly anchored, in Margarit's case, in the lessons of the quotidian. It is not surprising to hear Margarit distance himself from hermetic poetry, from mystical poetry (with its appeal to the ineffable), and from poetry drafted into the service of theology, philosophy, or any pursuit that diverts it from its primary purpose: the creation in the reader of a new sense of inner order. In Margarit's view, the reader enters the poem feeling emotional turmoil—fear, sadness, a sense of loss, whatever "threatens our inner harmony." If the poem is a good one, he or she will leave it feeling a new sense of clarity and calm—able to cope, a little better, with the chaos of the world. A bad poem, by contrast, "makes the world dirtier; it contributes to disorder, like a bag of rubbish left in the middle of the street."

But poetry's refuge, its "casa de misericordia," does not come already built. Poet and reader build it together. There is a distinct emphasis, in these pages, and throughout Margarit's work, on the reader's role in the creation of the poem—a role captured in "Archaic Torso of Apollo," which, like the letters, pays homage to Rilke. Looking at the statue,

> ...Each person contemplates the mirage,
> the cold eyes, the serene brow.
> All admire the strong hands
> without weapons, or with a haughty sword.
> All this beauty is marble of the air,
> a statue that can only exist
> the way each person imagines it.
> A poem is also that fragment
> seeking to be finished by others...

The association of poem and marble involves more than homage to Rilke. From the mid 1950s until his retirement a few years ago, Margarit was a practicing architect and a professor of calculation of structures in the Polytechnical University of Barcelona. Although he and his partner Carles Buxadé had dozens of major projects —parts of the campus of the Universitat Autonoma de Barcelona, the Montjüic Stadium for the Barcelona Olympics, the restoration of Gaudí's Palau Güell, work on the Sagrada Familia— he has written that he learned most from the inspections and structural repairs he performed on jerrybuilt apartment buildings erected during the Franco years to house a growing community of immigrants, in the suburbs of Barcelona, Lleida, and Tarragona. Each of those jobs involved a specific, often thorny structural problem and allowed Margarit to "submerge [himself], fleetingly, in the intimate lives of people in the outlying neighborhoods of a great city." As a a recent graduate in architecture and someone who was also writing his first poems, Margarit couldn't help but draw analogies between poetry and building—analogies which come into play both in his poems and in these *New Letters* and which involve an unapologetically rational poetics: his defensive reaction to the abiding presence of Romanticism and the Avant-Garde, whose "son" he recognizes himself to be. An important analogy—the one which gave rise to this little book—is that of the poetic *apprenticeship*, carried out in solitude (the fruitful solitude praised by Rilke). One of the lessons of that apprenticeship was the acknowledgment that rationality has its limits. In the prologue to one of his books Margarit writes that as a young architect he tended, in his calculations, to make his structures too robust: a lack of confidence in his own ability. Later, he went to the other extreme, making them too delicate. And then, in maturity, he distanced himself equally from both those positions, and learned "that there is no way that everything will be contained, ever, in any previous calculation." Not that the poet can ignore those calculations: for Margarit, it is no coincidence that the builder "tries to achieve the greatest resistance and stability with the least material possible (in general, steel or concrete) and that poetry tries to say the most with the fewest words."

As the reader will have sensed from these pages, architecture is not the only art which has helped shape Margarit's poetics. Music, too, has offered him aesthetic ideas, and consolations. He is an avid listener of jazz, has performed at festivals, and many of his poems, which tell a little story and unfurl like songs, have been set to music, by Joan Manuel Serrat and others. Although he remarks ironically that it adds nothing to a poem to say that it has "musical" properties (better not to demand "musicality of the word" and "go directly to Beethoven," Charlie Parker, or Coltrane), music is a constant presence in his life and work, as are the visual arts. It was while standing as a child before another sculpture in marble, *Els primers freds* (First Colds), by Miquel Blay, that it dawned on Margarit "that art is not different from life." Hours of looking at the paintings of Isidre Nonell—"as important for my work as Baudelaire"—taught him to "search for strength through humility—the only path that can lead to the poem." In one of his later books, inspired by etching, he wants to offer "scenes immobilized in emotional memory, in black and white or sepia," with the fewest possible words, and the least obtrusive "rhetorical resources."

Again, the emphasis on concision. In his most recent statements on poetry Margarit has spoken of his attempts to strip his poems of anything inessential and the belief that his usual mode of composition—he writes the same poem twice, first in Catalan and then, "almost at the same time," in Castilian— helps him achieve that simplicity.

> When I write the poem both in Castilian and Catalan [...] I am better able to locate all that is superfluous. Each of these languages detects more easily certain kinds of elements that are unneeded in a poem—whether words, images, verses, etc. Superimposing the two languages helps leave the poem in its most naked and elemental form.

His "superposition" of languages has affected not only the revision of individual poems but the shape of Margarit's oeuvre.

In gathering his poems into single volumes of selected verse, like *El primer frío / Els primers freds*, entire books—some of which have won major literary prizes—have fallen by the wayside. He is an implacable critic of his own work: "One of the signs by which I recognized my maturity as a poet was in the ability to disdain verses which, though brilliant, were not absolutely needed." He behaved the same way toward poems and books of poems: whatever could no longer console or commemorate, for commemoration is another major goal of his poems (one of the collections is titled *Architectures of Memory*):

> To leave proof of what one has felt at a given moment or to try to keep that moment from being worn away by time is one of the most elemental of defenses against the anguish we feel over the fleeting nature of our life. As Darwin wrote [of a pile of stones he had seen both in Wales and in South America]

"The desire to signalize any event, on the highest point of neighboring land, seems an universal passion with mankind." Each poem "signalizes" an event in my life, but my intention in writing it goes beyond that. Its ultimate purpose is to find a reader, in some other place, who can read it and realize that it is he or she who has placed a heap of stones on some high point of his or her own life, to signal some inner episode.

New Letters to a Young Poet commemorates such an "inner episode"—a young poet's encounter with Rilke—and draws lessons, many years later. The initial revelation is followed here by reflection, the desire to guide others and to share whatever clarity, whatever order and shelter poetry can provide.

—Christopher Maurer
Brookline, June 2010

Notes

Spanish text. I have translated from the revised Spanish text kindly sent to me by the author, and have also consulted two earlier versions: the first edition in Catalan, *Noves cartes a un jove poeta* (Proa, Els llibres de l'Osa Menor, 2009) and the first edition in Castilian, *Nuevas cartas a un poeta joven* (Barcelona: Barril & Barral Editores, 2010; first ed. 2009). For translations from Margarit's poetry in the notes that follow, I thank Anna Crowe, translator of three of Margarit's books.

P. 3 Edition of Rilke. Rilke has been a constant presence in Catalan and in Spanish poetry and poetics. The 1957 reprint to which Margarit is referring, translated with commentary by Guillermo Thiel and Luis di Iorio and first published in Buenos Aires in 1941, is one of many translations into Spanish of *Briefe an einen jungen Dichter.* The book has also been translated by Manuel Cardenal de

Iracheta (a selection in 1944 in *Escorial* in a special issue devoted to Rilke); A. Assa Anavi (1st ed. 1949); José María Valverde (1980); Antoni Pascual i Piqué and Constanza Bernad Ribera (1996); Elena Cortada de la Rosa (1999); Eustaquio Barjau and Joan Parra (2000); Jesús Munárriz (2004); Bernardo Ruiz (2006); and Linda Spahni (2009). Several of these translations have gone through multiple editions. The catalogue of the National Library of Argentina lists another fourteen. A heavily underlined page from Margarit's copy of the Thiel/di Iorio edition is reproduced at the end of the first edition of *Nuevas cartas*, along with a photograph of the poet at Rilke's grave. When he describes the book as his vademecum in a poetic "wilderness" he is thinking, perhaps, of T.S. Eliot ("Burnt Norton") and Cernuda ("Desolación de la quimera").

P. 8. First book. *Cantos para la coral de un hombre solo*, with a "Salutación" (greeting) by the novelist Camilo José Cela and drawings by the sculptor and printmaker Josep Maria Subirachs was published by Pere Vicens in 1963 in the publishing firm, Vicens Vives, which Vicens had founded two years earlier.

P. 8. Ocnos. In the mid-70s, the Colección Ocnos, created and directed by Spanish poet and professor Joaquín Marco, was the publisher of José Angel Valente, Homero Aridjis, Alejandra Pizarnik, Gabriel Celaya, Juan Gil-Albert, José María Valverde, and a number of other important Spanish and Latin American poets.

P. 9. The act of construction. In one of his books Margarit writes that, although he has been involved in some major projects, "my poems speak above all of another kind of architecture that I have never ceased to carry out. I refer to the rehabilitation and strengthening of buildings put up in the fifties and sixties—usually badly—in the outlying districts of Barcelona to house waves of immigrants, mainly from Andalucía. All those mornings and visits on-site to La Pau, Sant Roc, Parera, Turó de La Peira or El Besòs, were a series of technical problems that never got into the textbooks, of difficult decisions, emergencies, and bars with coffee laced with brandy. On all those mornings I wrote a large part of my poetry, while I was learning my profession as an architect just as much as when I went to those other sites that seemed more important." *Barcelona, amor final* (Barcelona: Proa, 2007): p. 327; tr. Anna Crowe.)

P. 10. Rilke: "those mysterious...": *Letters to a Young Poet*, translated and with a foreword by Stephen Mitchell (New York: Vintage Books), p. 4; rejection of Kappus's texts as poems, p. 5; "whether you would have to die", p. 6.

P. 13. Even Larkin's poetry... letter to Robert Lowell, July 30, 1964 in *Words in Air: The Complete Correspondence Between Elizabeth Bishop and Robert Lowell*, ed. Thomas Travisano and Saskia Hamilton (New York: Farrar, Straus and Giroux, 2008): 547.

P. 15. Outer reality: Rilke (11) advises Kappus that he couldn't disturb [his growth] any more violently than by looking outside and waiting for outside answers to questions that only [his] innermost feeling, in [his] quietest hour, can perhaps answer."

P. 21. Gabriel Ferrater (1922–72), whom Margarit considers "one of the central figures in the modern tradition of love poetry in Catalan" (*Poesía amorosa completa 1980–2000*, Barcelona, Proa, 2001, p. 11), and to whom he devotes an elegy (*Barcelona amor final*, p. 355) remarked in an interview that "A poem has to begin by having at least as much sense as a business letter. It should have a lot more sense, but it must begin with at least that. If it has less, it no longer exists as a poem." *Papers, cartes, paraules,* ed. Joan Ferraté (Barcelona: Edicions dels Quaderns Crema, 1986): 521. With Pere Rovira, Margarit translated from Catalan into Castilian Ferrater's *Poema inacabat* (Unfinished Poem) (Madrid: Alianza Editorial, 1989).

P. 24. Coromines. According to the etymological dictionary of Joan Coromines and José Antonio Pascual (Madrid: Gredos, 1980), *s.v. letra*, the word literatura first appears in a Spanish dictionary in 1490.

P. 24. Intellectuals and poets. Rilke, too, advises Kappus to "read as little as possible of literary criticism" (22).

P. 26. José Antonio Coderch de Sentmenat (1913–1984). "He was my master," Margarit writes. "His concept of art has stamped all my thinking, not only on architecture, but also on poetry." Cf. his "Elegía para el arquitecto Coderch de Sentmenat": "He said that architecture cannot disturb, that it must please / the guest passing through on his way to other abodes, who rests in the rooms. / He said the house should be virtuous and humble, it should not be / independent, made in vain, original, sumptuous." *Barcelona amor final*, p. 263.

P. 26. Segimon Serrallonga (1930-2002), humanist, poet, cultural activist and educator; translator of Blake and Brecht, and from classical, German, American and other literatures. In "Llegir els clàssics amb Riba," Serrallonga studies Riba's interpretation of the classical world.

P. 28. Stefan Zweig. In his Abschied von Rilke, 1927, Zweig remarks how "inexplicable" it is "that in the midst of a thousand dull men, only one ever turns Poet; nor can it be explained why it was just this One of us all and at just this temporal moment." See *Farewell to Rilke*, tr. Marion Sonnenfeld (New York: State University College, 1975): 1.

P. 29. Thoughts on translation. Margarit has translated, with Sam Abrams, 170 poems of Thomas Hardy and the complete poetry of Elizabeth Bishop. He has also translated poems by, among others, Czesław Miłosz and (with Anna Crowe) R.S. Thomas.

P. 31. Voltaire. The reference is probably to *Commentaire sur Corneille* (p. 953): "Il ne faut pas dire: je pleure, il faut que par vos discours on juge que votre coeur et déchiré." *Oeuvres complètes de Voltaire* eds. Ulla Kölving et al (Genève, Banbury, Oxford, Voltaire Foundation, 1968-), Vol. 54: 953.

P. 33. Soledad sonora. Literally "resonant solitude" or "melodious solitude," from "Cántico espiritual." The phrase was used by Juan Ramón Jiménez as the title of one of his books (1912), for which Margarit wrote a prologue in 2007. *Jacint Verdaguer* (1845–1902): The comment that Verdaguer had an "abyss" behind him alludes to his pioneering role in the revival of poetry in Catalan, which had been little cultivated in the nineteenth century. Although he was an ordained priest, Verdaguer is better known for his epic *Atlántida* (on which Manuel de Falla based a cantata) than for his religious poetry.

P. 33. The Catalan poet Joan Vinyoli (1914–1984), author of 17 books of poems. To *The Notebooks of Malte Laurids Brigge*, Vinyoli attributes his own discovery that "poems are not—as people think—feelings; they are experiences"; a distinction important to Margarit. See Ferrán Carbó, *Introducció a la poesia de Joan Vinyoli* (Barcelona: Publicacions de l'Abadia de Montserrat. 1991): 9.

P. 35. Benjamín. "Surrealism: The Last Snapshot of the European Intelligentsia" in *Selected Writings, Volume 2 1927–1934*, tr. by Rodney Livingstone and others; edited by Michael W. Jennings, Howard Eiland, and Gary Smith (Cambridge: Belknap Press of Harvard University Press, 1999): 218.

P. 35. Very boring poem. See Martin Heidegger, *Hölderlin's Hymn "The Ister".* Tr. William McNeil and Julia Davis (Bloomington: Indiana University Press, 1996.)

P. 36. Miquel Bauçà (1934–2004), poet and author of essays and aphorisms. Two lines in "Ultimos combates" (Final Struggles) testify to that feeling: "They were bored, both by Franco in the newspapers / and Marx in the underground meetings" (*Barcelona, amor final*, p. 283)

P. 36. Cabra. Lorca comments on the song in "How a City Sings from November to November." See *A Season in Granada: Uncollected Poems and Prose*, tr. Christopher Maurer (London: Anvil Press Poetry, 1998): 102–04. Margarit's listeners in Cabra had never heard of the song or, of course, the recording of La Argentinita singing it, with Lorca at the piano.

P. 40. The classics. The least known in the U.S. is the Valencian Vicent Andrés Estellés (1924–1993), despite David H. Rosenthal's *Nights That Make The Night: Selected Poems* (New York: Persea Books, 1992). In "Comentario de texto," from his collection *Mysteriously Happy*, Margarit comments ironically on Estellés's poem "Los amantes," reflects on the genre of love poetry, and pokes fun at the line: "No había dos amantes como tú y yo en Valencia" ("There were never two lovers in Valencia like you and me.") *Misteriosamente feliz* (Madrid: Visor Poesía, 2009): 83. An engaging essay by Sam Abrams on love poetry in Catalan, with comments on Estellés, serves as introduction to Margarit's *Poesía amorosa completa* (see pp. 19–21).

P. 41. Love is a crowded city. Admiring allusion to a poem by Agustí Batra, "Amor, ciutat voltada de verds símbols terrestres..." (see Abrams, p. 17).

P. 45. "I conceived it..." Translated by Anna Crowe. Original in *Casa de Misericordia* (Barcelona: Edicions Proa, 2007): 82–83.

P. 46. Bad poem. Els primers freds. Poesia 1975–1995 (Edicions Proa, 2004): 14.

P. 47. "Archaic Torso of Apollo": in Catalan in *Els primers freds,* p. 229; and, more concisely, in Spanish in *El primer frío* (Madrid: Visor, 2004). I have translated this fragment from the Spanish.

P: 48. "Say the most with the fewest words": Interview with José Luis Morante, in Antonio Jiménez Millán, ed. *Amor y tiempo. La poesía de Joan Margarit* (Córdoba: Ediciones Litopress, 2005): 142.

P. 48. Musicality. See Margarit's prologue to Juan Ramón Jiménez, *La soledad sonora (1908)* (Madrid: Visor, 2007): 16.

P. 49. Etching. *El primer frío,* p. 371.

P. 49. Writing in Catalan and Castilian. Margarit describes his method of composition in a prologue to *Llegas tarde a tu tiempo. Poesía 1999–2002* (Madrid: Visor, 2002): 13. The quote is from Jiménez Millán, p. 143.

P. 50. Darwin, stones. El primer frío, p. 13. In his *Elizabeth Bishop. Obra poética* (co-translated with Sam Abrams) (Barcelona: Ediciones Igitur, 2008), Margarit notes that Bishop "achieves her best poems through an exactness and a harmony that owes more to the work of Darwin than to that of any poet" (p. 19).

Acknowledgments

The author thanks Mariona Ribalta and Jordi Gracia for their intelligent critical suggestions during the writing of these letters. The translator is grateful for the help and trust of Joan Margarit and David Rade.

Swan Isle Press is an independent, not-for-profit, literary publisher
dedicated to publishing works of poetry, fiction and nonfiction that
inspire and educate while advancing the knowledge and appreciation
of literature, art, and culture. The Press's bilingual editions and
single-language English translations make contemporary and
classic texts more accessible to a variety of readers.
For information on books of related interest or for
a catalog of new publications contact:
www.swanislepress.com

New Letters to a Young Poet

Designed by Esmeralda Morales-Guerrero
Typeset in Calluna
Printed on 55# Glatfelter Natural